Organizing and Operating Profitable Workshop Classes

by

Janet Ruhe-Schoen

Organizing and Operating Profitable Workshop Classes

by
Janet Ruhe-Schoen

PILOT BOOKS • NEW YORK

Library of Congress Catalog Card Number: 80-25466

Library of Congress Cataloging in Publication Data

Ruhe-Schoen, Janet.
  Organizing and operating profitable workshop
classes.

  1. Workshops (Adult education)—Handbooks, manuals,
etc. I. Title.
LC44.R83   374'.29   80-25446
ISBN 0-87576-092-9

Printed in United States of America

ABOUT THE AUTHOR

Janet Ruhe-Schoen is a professional writer and editor who has personally operated a series of home workshops.

CONTENTS

Page

Why This Book Was Written 7

What Will You Teach? 9

Who Will You Teach? 10

Where Will You Teach? 14

The Curriculum 16

Teaching Hints 18

What To Charge 21

Promoting Your Workshop 22

Signing Up Students 28

Record Keeping 30

WHY THIS BOOK WAS WRITTEN

Are you expert at woodcarving, weaving, acting, chess, playing an instrument, dancing, collecting coins or any other skill that you consider "just a hobby?"

If you are, this book will show you how to turn this expertise into a pleasant, fulfilling way of earning extra money. If you know and enjoy your subject, and are ready to enthusiastically share your knowledge, you can organize and teach workshop classes.

You'll be starting a profitable small business of your own, and have the satisfaction of working with people who want to learn.

Chapter One

What Will You Teach?

Your first step is to decide what you want to teach. Here are just some subjects which can form the basis of profitable workshops:

Accounting

Appliance Repair

Art—Painting, Sculpture, Drawing, Printmaking

Astrology

Auto Mechanics

Ballroom, Ballet, Folk, and/or Belly Dancing

Business Skills

Candle-making

Carpentry

Ceramics

Chess

Collecting (art, antiques, collectibles)

Crocheting, Knitting, Needlepoint, Embroidery, Sewing

Dramatics

Framing

Furniture Building, Refinishing, Restoration

Gardening

Gourmet Cooking

Home Maintenance

Investments

Languages

Mime

Musical Instruments

Nursing Skills

Pet Care and Grooming

Photography

Puppetry

Quilting

Speechmaking

Starting a Business

Typing

Weaving

Writing

Voice

Wine Tasting and Selection

Yoga

The list could be much longer. With the correct approach, almost any subject can attract eager students.

Chapter Two

Who Will You Teach?

Suppose your talent seems especially geared to a certain age group, but you don't want to teach that age group? For instance, you can make beautiful puppets and give funny puppet shows, but you really don't want to give workshops for children.

You could collect a group of interested adults. Many people are interested in learning puppetry so that they can work with children, or just because they are interested for themselves. Most adults love a chance to perform. If they complete the workshop by giving a puppet show for the public or a special group, they will be thrilled, and so will you.

On the other hand, suppose you have a "grown-up" skill like mechanics, but you love working with kids. Try teaching them how to repair their own bicycles. Many children also would enjoy learning chess, sewing, knitting, and other skills you may think are only for adults.

Don't limit yourself. Find yourself a group of students you'll enjoy. You may even decide to teach adults and children together.

TEACHING ADULTS

An informative, informal approach is successful with adults. They are your peers who share an interest with you, and some of them may become your good friends. They will, at first, regard you with a critical eye. It is important that you be well-organized and self-confident.

The old adage stands: be yourself. If you are bouncy and bubbly, don't try to be austere and dignified. If you are reserved, don't try to become a comedian. If you are slightly messy and tend to have ink on your fingers most of the time, don't start getting a weekly manicure just to impress your students.

Being well-organized and self-confident comes from knowing your material and knowing what you want your students to learn. You will then teach well, and your students will be satisfied.

TEACHING CHILDREN

You must prove to adults that you have a firm grip on your subject. You must prove to children not only that you have a firm grip on your subject, but you also have a firm grip on them.

You can be informal and relaxed with children. In fact, it is important to have a sense of humor and share it with them. They will test you to find out how authoritative you are, and you must be firm.

Most children will be cooperative from the first. They are there because they are interested. A few may be there just because mommy thinks they would like it. They would rather be playing outdoors. They can easily be won over when they see that you are no fool and the classes are fun. Those who arrive with a ready eagerness will be disappointed if you don't immediately teach them new things; like adults, they may regard you critically.

So get your children involved at once in an interesting project. Once they are interested, misbehavior stops. For instance, Joe may begin the first class by constantly pulling Mary's pigtails, and Mary may encourage Joe by screaming and kicking him. Calmly tell them to stop. Continue introducing the activity. If Joe and Mary don't stop, separate them.

Don't waste time being a judge, trying to figure out who started it. Don't try to reason with Joe, trying to convince him to be a good boy. Just go on with the class business. Say, "I'm not here to play police. I'm here to help you make puppets, so let's get started." Children only act up when they are bored or are testing your authority; some may begin each class with a little test, but don't let such thorns stick in your side. You'll soon learn enough about each child to handle the class well.

If a child is impossible to deal with it may be because of emotional problems. Don't try to be a therapist. Talk to the parents about the child and see if you can get some insights that will help you. If the child is too difficult to handle ask the parents to take the boy or girl from the class.

Let the children talk, laugh, and help each other while working. Your class should be very different from their public school experience. If it is, you may find that some children who are regarded by others as having problems are very well-adjusted while with you.

As with adults, let the children share their skills. Encourage them to praise each other and help each other. Let them talk and laugh while working, but don't feel that you must put up with intolerable noise.

Children are extremely inventive if allowed to be, and you may learn many new things from them and get a lot of ideas. If you demonstrate one way of putting something together, and notice Sue doing it another way, let her go. She may have found a way that is better than yours. Or she may have to learn that your way is best.

11

It is most important that the children feel they are having fun. Children are fun addicts. So are adults, but the difference is that children like to feel, at the beginning of a workshop, that it is play and, by the end of it, that it is good work. Adults like to begin by feeling that they are working very hard. At the end, they realize that they are also playing.

When teaching children you have two groups of people to please: the children and the parents. The children are process-oriented, the parents product-oriented. In other words, children love the process of making something or learning something; for example, messing about with finger paints, finding out that red and blue make purple and too many colors together make mud. Parents, however, don't appreciate their child's mud-colored painting. They want to see a pretty painting by their child. Sometimes, they want the child's work to look as if an adult did it.

You need to compromise. A child will, of course, take pride in a pretty painting for which he or she mixed pretty colors; or at least in a representational painting which may not be pretty but is, at least, recognizable as a horrible monster. Parents can also appreciate such paintings. However, no child is proud of a piece of work that the teacher worked over to make it look "perfect." Parents don't want to see the teacher's work, either.

Let the children enjoy their process. Encourage them to be playful and experimental. Don't scold if they end up with an awkward-looking project. Just give them a goal they can meet. When they meet it, the parents will understand what you have been doing.

For instance, at the end of an art workshop you can hang up each child's paintings from the first one to the last, so their progress is clearly discernible.

Children are hard to teach because they have in their own minds, complete and glittering, whatever they want to express. It may, however, look like a wiggly red house in a field of manila paper. Your task is to subtly guide them toward an external, understandable expression of what is so clear in their own minds. It is possible to do this, with varying degrees, with children from the ages of about 6 and up. Don't even expect to begin it with tiny ones. They live in their imaginary worlds and most parents of pre-schoolers are pleased if their little ones are just having fun and being happy with other children.

In teaching such small children, your basic task is to love them, enjoy them, give them brief and simple projects. Make them happy, and they'll make you very happy!

TEACHING TEENAGERS

Treat teenagers like adults unless they act like children. Most of them will be in your class by their own volition. Some may arrive via their own transportation, and pay with their own money. Most will be cooperative unless you let them down.

Some immature teens may test your authority by being slightly rude. If you don't assert your authority, you will lose the respect of the whole class. Don't overreact and snap at them, or make sarcastic remarks. Just say, "I'd like your attention so we can get on with our work."

Once interest is established, the class is yours. Teenagers are very enjoyable to teach. Their minds are fairly mature, they have adult coordination and some knowledge of life, yet they have youthful spontaneity and enthusiasm. Even teenagers who seem extremely cool and jaded have a wonderful eagerness once their interest is captured.

More than with any age group, it is imperative that you be yourself with teenagers. They hate fakes. Don't try to be one of them or impress them with how hip you are. Share your subject with enthusiasm and they'll follow along.

Chapter Three

Where Will You Teach?

If you have a large recreation room or other suitable area in your home, you're set; no rent.

If your home isn't large enough, look for the cheapest possible place that is still attractive. Some libraries, churches and synagogues have large rooms that they rent for a small fee. Also, try the town hall, American Legion, Elks, Masonic Temple, schools, etc. You'll surely find something.

Stay away from commercial office space. You'll usually have to sign a lease and pay a fairly high rent. Look for community groups who will be happy to have the small fee you pay as a contribution to their activities.

Perhaps you will be offered a large room, shed, or yard that would be suitable. Even if it is offered to you free of charge, insist on paying for it or returning the favor in some other concrete way. Be sure that you clearly define the use of the space and your responsibilities in case of damages.

Remember if a space is large enough, you can temporarily transform it to meet your requirements. With a wooden platform, and some portable lights, you can create a theatrical environment. It would be helpful if there is a cabinet or closet which you can use for storage so you and your students don't have to lug easels, lights, potting soil, etc. back and forth every week. If there is no storage space, you can supply an old set of shelves, or large boxes from the supermarket—whatever is cheap and meets your needs. Use your ingenuity.

For some workshops, you need a very specific environment. You need a darkroom for photography; a workroom with a potter's wheel for ceramics; a shop for woodwork, etc. You may be able to use your home workspace, but if it isn't feasible, don't despair. See if you can use an equipped room in a school, "Y" or similar organization. You may even end up instructing as a faculty member of that institution.

Even if you can't find inside space you can still find a way around the problem. You can teach "Photo Vision," for instance, working outside with cameras. Don't be too much of a perfectionist and you'll think of a way to teach some aspect of your craft. If you're a good teacher, you'll give your students the essentials without getting wrapped up in a lot of technical details.

WORKSHOP FURNISHINGS

First of all, you need seats. If you rent space, most rooms or halls come equipped with benches or folding chairs. If this is lacking, be sure to check further. Seating is probably stored somewhere in the building. Tables of various sizes may also be available.

If you must provide your own tables and chairs, see if you can borrow them or get them as cheaply as possible at yard sales, used furniture outlets or thrift shops. If you want your students to be able to sit on the floor and it is uncarpeted, you can get carpet remnants or throw rugs from the same sources.

Think thrift. For instance, you may think you need a blackboard, and the room does not have one. Try using a large newsprint drawing pad propped on a chair and make your illustrations with a felt-tipped marker. Until you teach a class or two, you really can't be sure how much you'll use certain supplies. Buy as little as possible until you know exactly what you need.

For adult classes, it is nice to have a coffee-maker or hot plate to heat water for coffee and tea. Your students will really appreciate it.

Chapter Four

The Curriculum

Now that you know what you will teach, and to whom, decide how you will teach. It's simplest to point the workshop toward a goal: completion of a project. Each student will be most satisfied by ending the workshop with an accomplishment: a well-made table; playing jazz progressions on the guitar; the ability to meditate for five minutes; or starting a business.

Think of what gave you the greatest sense of accomplishment when you were first learning your skill. Outline a curriculum with that accomplishment as the goal.

Refer to some current books on the particular subject. It's also good to brush up a bit, just to get new ideas.

Figure out how much time your students will need. Can they reach the goal with one two-hour session per week for four weeks, or will one hour be sufficient? It is probably best to make your first workshop a four or six week one for beginning students. That is enough of a challenge for a novice teacher.

Don't draw up a detailed curriculum. A simple structure with a definite goal is enough. As you work with your students, you will get ideas for effective teaching.

Here is an example of a simple workshop curriculum: The subject: *Acting for Teenagers*. Each class is two hours long. The goal: *to help each student learn a bit about characterization.*

Week 1: Warm up . . . (Theater games). Improvised skits.

Week 2: Warm up . . . improvisation using only pantomime.

Week 3: Warm up . . . pantomime improvisation using hats, props, costumes to inspire characterization . . . solo work with characters in various situations.

Week 4: Warm up . . . work on characters from week 3, adding speech only at stress points (improvise scenes with characters in pairs and/or groups)

Week 5: Warm up . . . help students make up as their characters. Explore effects of lighting. Improvise scenes in make up with lights.

Week 6: In-class recital—families & friends invited to provide audience . . . warm up as usual, then present characters in improvised scenes, pantomime or with speech. Finish with special refreshments.

As you may imagine, this curriculum could change depending on the abilities of the students, but it does give the teacher a definite starting point and a goal. No matter how advanced or unskilled the students are, if the teacher sticks to the goal, they will finish with a definite sense of accomplishment.

SCHEDULING

Scheduling is simple. Just decide the time and day. Pick a time when you'll be alert and refreshed. If Wednesday is your most hectic day, don't plan a class for Wednesday evening.

When you pick a time stick with it. Constant changes of schedule will irritate your students. Never change a class time or cancel the class unless a real emergency arises, in which case you'll find that most people are extremely understanding.

If you have the flu on Wednesday and your class is on Thursday evening, don't wait until Thursday afternoon to see if you feel well enough to teach. When you call people at the last minute, some will get annoyed. It's safer to notify your students of the cancellation on Wednesday. Then schedule a make-up session so your students will have all the classes they paid for.

THE LAST CLASS

It is good to have something special at or after the last class—a party, a play, a show, a field trip. If you have geared the whole workshop toward some sort of display or play, your students will, of course, be ready. Leave details up to them. For instance, if they want to charge admission, let them use it for what they wish, whether it be for a party or to make a charitable donation. It's theirs; your profit is their tuition.

For another type of workshop, you may just want to bring up the idea of how to end it as you near the last class. The students may want to do a little recital just for family and friends, but not for the public. Or they may want to bring their families to a little class party, or go as a class to a play or museum. Be ready to suggest various activities, but do exactly what they want.

If they have signed up knowing they'll do a play, for instance, and then get weak-kneed about it, don't back down. Make sure they do it; they'll feel like heroes afterwards.

Chapter Five

Teaching Hints

The most effective teaching technique for any age group is PRAISE.

People learn more from being praised than they do from being criticized. After words of praise, a person is open to learning. After criticism, a person usually tightens up and withdraws.

For instance, suppose you are teaching quilting. Julia sews a fine line but has no color sense, and her squares are badly mismatched. Heather matches fabrics beautifully and sews miserably. You praise Julia's sewing and ask her how she does it. You praise Heather's color craft and ask her how she does it. You don't have to say anything that is even slightly negative.

If Julia and Heather just say they don't know, it's natural to them, then you, having observed Julia's use of her needle and Heather's experiments with and final placing of fabrics, explain how they do it. Each will have learned from the other without a word of criticism. Each will have pride in her own ability.

THE FIRST CLASS

Your first class sets the pattern for the rest. It should be lively and pleasant. Your students should leave feeling they have learned something new, and that they are part of a congenial group. This will make them eager to return.

You create this feeling by being relaxed, friendly, and alert to student needs. Give them a project which will show you their abilities and enable you to give them a few pointers. Of course you can't immediately get to know them very well. Some may be shy and will need a few classes before they really can be natural and relaxed. At the first class, you will, however, be able to see who is shy, who needs more sensitive handling, who is overbearing, who is advanced in the skill and who is completely ignorant of it.

Don't just chat and have coffee at the first class, and assume you are getting acquainted. Your students want to learn; put them to work.

Have them work together to create a feeling of camaraderie. For example, if you're teaching portraiture, have partners draw each other, instead of everyone drawing one person. Then post the portraits and offer refreshments while each person comments on the portraits. Ask them to praise the best points in each portrait. Then you cap the session with some illuminating comments and perhaps a demonstration. Your students will be eager to get together again.

THINKING CREATIVELY

With creative thought, you can effectively introduce any subject. Thinking creatively means thinking in terms of ACTION.

If you explain something, a student may see your point, but if you have the students DO something, they will understand and remember your point. In other words, it's helpful to discuss what happens at antique auctions if you are teaching a class in collecting, but your students will really learn if you accompany them to an auction. Translate every concept you want to teach into activity for the students.

Always stay alert during class; don't sit down and read while the students are working. Circulate among them, observing. Don't start on your own project unless you can do it without becoming too self-involved! Be sure you praise a student whenever you notice improvement; you may be surprised to find that the student was absolutely unaware of improvement, and needed the encouragement.

Don't be afraid to let the class go a bit overtime, or to spend a little time with a student after class. Your students will appreciate your patience. If you give your best, the students themselves will build your reputation by word-of-mouth.

You do not have to know all the answers. Do not pretend you do. You are providing a space, a forum, a structure for learning. You are a resource person with a fund of specific knowledge. If one of your students is enthusiastic about a book you never heard of, or possesses an instinctive flair you lack, or knows a new little twist or technique, be grateful for the opportunity to learn yourself.

REFRESHMENTS

It helps to have tea and coffee for adults, and some juice for children. Cookies and other snacks are also nice. During most adult classes, people will just help themselves when they feel like it, but it's best to declare a certain time for a break.

During a children's class, have a definite refreshment time. You serve the snacks, or supervise children who want to serve them. Even if the class lasts only an hour and the refreshment is just some juice, it's a nice touch.

You can suggest that your older students or youngster's parents contribute snack foods, but don't make them feel they must. You provide the basics. People often like to bake things and bring them to class when it is going well. No doubt you'll enjoy special treats at the last class.

Chapter Six

What To Charge

How much is your time and knowledge worth? If you are accomplished enough to teach others the basics of a skill, you should consider yourself a professional and be paid as such.

This does not mean that each student must pay you an exorbitant fee. In fact, workshops are attractive to students because individual fees are usually reasonable. Consider: if you have 10 students coming once a week to a two hour session, and your workshop runs for six sessions, and each student pays $5.00 per hour, you will be earning $50.00 per hour, or $100.00 per class. The complete session will gross $600.00 less whatever rent you pay and any other overhead, such as expenses for refreshments, printing flyers, etc., which should be very low.

The cost to each student is only $60.00 for the whole workshop. That is an extremely attractive charge. The lower the fee, the more students you'll have. And the more students you have, the more popular your workshops will become.

Don't underestimate your potential. A national magazine recently cited an example of a man and his wife who run art instruction workshops in their home. They charge $120 per student for twelve weekly 1½ hour sessions, and also offer private lessons. Their workshops have proven to be very successful.

People generally dislike being part of a very small class; they prefer a class of about 10 participants. Don't let the class become too large either. If there is that much interest, form two units.

Chapter Seven

Promoting Your Workshop

When you've figured out what, who, how, when, and where to teach, what you'll need and how much you'll charge, it's time to announce your workshops.

POSTERS AND FLYERS

You can make posters and put one on every bulletin space in town; that means boards, walls, and store windows. Create places for your posters by asking libraries, schools, and merchants to post them.

You don't have to be an artist to make an attractive poster. First, decide what you want to say. You want to announce your workshops as simply and clearly as possible. Don't give all the details on the poster; people don't read fine print or cramped copy. You'll give full information to people who call. A successful poster arouses curiosity, but does not satisfy it.

To make a poster, take a piece of white typing paper, a pencil, and a ruler. Measure one inch margins on top, bottom, and sides of the paper and rule them in lightly with the pencil. Mark the exact center of the paper and rule it with a pencil line. Make lines on which to write, ½ inches apart, the length of the paper. In large, legible letters write your message in pencil. Then go over it with a black, narrow felt-tipped marker. Make your letters as dark as possible.

If you want to illustrate your poster, but you can't draw, try using a black and white glossy photograph of yourself or someone else participating in the activity you'll be teaching.

If you are not satisfied with your lettering, you can use stencils or paste-down lettering which you buy in an art supply store. What you are doing is preparing camera ready art for an offset printer. Take your copy to a quick print place and have 50 or 100 printed. In fact, if you just can't make the poster yourself, such places usually have a graphic artist on hand who can design it for you fairly cheaply. The printing cost for 100 copies will probably be around $5.00. Get more if necessary. Post them everywhere. Don't forget office buildings, railroad sta-

puppet workshops

for: ages 6-7 • ages 8-10 • ages 11-13

MAKiNG PUPPETS AND PUPPET PLAYS

for more information, ☎ call:
876-2628 (please call by Oct. 17)

tions, religious and fraternal organizations, as well as churches and synagogues.

Use the poster as a circular and put a few on the counters of banks, libraries—any place with available counter space. If you're teaching woodworking, a hardware store may distribute your circulars; an art supply store may help you advertise art classes.

You can distribute circulars among the members of any organization you belong to. If you will be teaching children, the school might let you distribute them among the students. However, since you are not a non-profit organization, the school administration may prefer to simply let you place a poster on the bulletin board.

PRESS RELEASES

Announce your workshop in the local newspaper with a press release, which is a news item. For example:

PETER PEPPER
Address
Telephone Number
Person's name to contact

For Immediate Release

Peter Pepper is now accepting enrollments for his course in mouth-watering bread-baking. Basic quick breads and yeast breads will be baked and consumed, including the fluffy delights of croissants, brioches, and anisette biscuits.

Pepper's kitchen at 9 New Garden Street is large and warm and open to the first ten prospective bakers who call 999-0909 by September 19th.

# # #

The newspaper may rewrite your release, making it seem dry and tasteless to you, but don't be discouraged. All the readers really need to know is what the workshop is about and who they can call for information. The newspaper will appreciate it if your release is as brief as possible.

Bring the release to the paper yourself; don't mail it the first time. You want to introduce yourself to the editor or to the editor of the relevant section of the paper. For instance, you should bring a release about cooking classes to the editor of the daily living section. You and your workshop may be so interesting that the editor will want to do a human interest feature on you, including some of your recipes. Local newspapers frequently run articles featuring interesting home-town folks. You couldn't get better publicity.

OTHER OUTLETS FOR PRESS RELEASES

Send a release to every newspaper in your area, not just the largest one. Bulletins put out by special interest groups, such as churches, parent-teacher associations, art councils should all receive a press release. In some areas, special advertising publications, which include a "what's going on" section are delivered to every home on a weekly basis. Be sure to include them on your list.

DEMONSTRATIONS AND DISPLAYS

Demonstrate your skill or display your products, if possible. Religious groups, clubs, libraries, local tv stations and schools often seek special programs. Don't feel shy about announcing your workshops during your demonstration. Interested people will appreciate it. If you put up a display in a library, school, bank, or downtown store window, be sure your name, phone number, and the fact that you give classes is included.

ADVERTISING

If you get ample publicity, you should have enough students to get started. It would probably be best to advertise only after you have given several successful workshops and want to build more classes.

NEWSPAPER DISPLAY AD

A display ad is the kind you commonly see throughout a newspaper. It is generally in a box and has drawings and/or large print to make it noticeable. It may be a full page, half page, quarter page, or a few inches deep. An extremely large ad can cost hundreds of dollars. A very small one is rarely noticed. Your best bet is to call your local newspaper, find out ad rates, and buy an ad that's as large as you can afford. It should be at least 2 column inches wide and 3 column inches long (4 inches by 6 inches).

Running the ad once is ineffective. You must run it a few weeks in a row if your paper is a weekly, every day for a week or every other day for two weeks if your paper is a daily. It will be expensive.

Keep the copy brief so the type can be as large as possible. You can give the paper a copy of your poster to use as an ad. This ad will stand out because it will be a different style from the rest of the paper. It can usually be reproduced in whatever size you specify.

If you find that you absolutely cannot afford to advertise in the leading local paper, you may be able to afford smaller, independent newspapers if they are available.

CLASSIFIED ADS

Classified ads are relatively inexpensive, and are often a well-read part of a newspaper. You can run an ad under ''Instruction'' for a week or so. Here again, don't neglect the smaller newspapers, especially those which may specialize in your field. For instance, in some towns entrepreneurs are publishing weekly guides to local entertainment, musical and otherwise, and they run classifieds. Some Arts Councils publish county-wide papers for members, in which any arts workshop could be well-publicized.

Classified ads are priced at a minimum charge. Check the rates and then examine the classified section in any paper for an idea of how to briefly word your ad.

Investigate all publications in your area to see where it would be best and most affordable to advertise.

THE YELLOW PAGES

Once you are really established, you can list your name under ''Music Instructor,'' ''Art Instruction'' or ''Schools'' in the yellow pages. The cost is not exorbitant and it is usually productive.

RADIO COMMERCIALS

If you were a nonprofit organization, you could be announced without charge on community news shows, but as you are not you will have to pay, and it costs.

Spot announcements on a popular radio station are extremely effective, but must be repeated frequently to get the message across, and you pay for the time. An ad person or D.J. at the station can help you make a tape for an ad, or can make the tape for you.

Choose an appropriate station. You'll find teenage students through rock stations, adults through easy-listening ones. Choose the best time slot. Select the time when you are most likely to reach your potential market.

Chapter Eight

Signing Up Students

The phone rings, you pick it up, a voice says "Are you the person giving the belly-dancing workshop?" and you're on.

Be assured and confident. Give the caller complete information on the schedule, fee and payment policy plus what he or she can expect to learn. Some people might ask you about your own experience level. Tell them frankly, and ask them about theirs. It will help you know (if you haven't specified that you will only teach a certain level) how many beginners and more advanced students you'll have.

If you have a very busy household, it may help to keep notes by the phone so that, in busy moments, you don't forget how much you're charging and impress a caller as being too muddle-minded to teach. If someone calls while you are extremely busy don't be afraid to say, "Please wait a minute" while you put things in order. You can then sit down and calmly discuss your workshop.

Keep a pencil and paper by the phone and note each student's name, address, phone number and experience level. Some people may want to talk at length, especially mothers who are enrolling their small children in drama or dance workshops. Let them talk; you might as well get used to it.

One of your callers may be very eager to take the class but may not have transportation. Tell the caller you'll phone later. By noting students' addresses you may, after all the calls are in, be able to arrange a ride.

Another person may be disappointed to find that he can't attend on the day you've chosen to have a class. Make a note. If enough other callers have the same trouble, perhaps you can change the time of the class. However, don't start trying to change the schedule for just one or two people. You can schedule your next workshop for a different time.

PAYMENT POLICY

It's best to have your students pay for the complete course at the first class. Give those who pay in cash a receipt and keep a duplicate copy for your records. Keep a record of those who pay with checks too.

It's better not to have the students pay at each session. That means if they are absent, they don't pay. Such a payment policy is unfair to you. You are using your time to prepare and teach classes and you should be paid for your time.

If someone attends one class and then, for some reason, must drop out, you will want to refund most of their balance. You should, however, establish a policy of no refunds after a certain number of classes.

You might run into a person who attends classes and keeps stating that you will be paid at the next class. If a participant does not pay after two sessions, they must bring the payment to the next class or drop the workshop. The student may have a real hard luck story. In that case, participation in your class can come later when it can be afforded.

However, if someone is low on cash but is eager to learn, you may want to work out a barter with them. Perhaps the person can pay you in goods or services instead of money.

SPECIAL SUPPLIES

If you need special equipment such as easels, music stands, etc., first see if your prospective students have them. Many probably will, and can use them in class. The others can borrow or buy their own. Try to recommend an inexpensive source.

If something like a small loom is needed, you may want to help students make their own. The point is to do things as economically as possible. If your class is building something, find out where they can obtain the materials and give them detailed directions on what to get.

Some things, however, definitely should be supplied by you. Students should not be asked to pay for a puppet stage, lighting fixtures, a platform for the figure-drawing model, or anything permanent that can be used by many students, in many workshops.

Students should bring things which they will use to make their projects, such as wood, clay, fabric scraps, etc. Keep paper and pen on hand for those who forget to bring their own for taking notes. You may want to mimeograph or photocopy certain information for them.

Chapter Nine

Record Keeping

Check with your lawyer to determine your exact legal responsibilities. Be sure to conform with local zoning laws and see whether you need any kind of a business license. This information is available from your county, village or city clerk as well as the local license bureau.

Work out a simple bookkeeping system with your accountant. It is essential that you keep accurate records for tax purposes. Be certain to carefully determine whether you will be eligible to deduct the appropriate part of your utility and phone expenses as well as a percentage of your rent or monthly home costs.

Your lawyer or insurance agent can provide you with information regarding any special coverage you may need to protect yourself since you will be dealing with the public.

This may seem to be a nuisance, as well as time-consuming, but starting a business is never completely simple.

CONCLUSION

You now have the basics for starting an interesting, profitable part- or full-time workshop business.

Running any business demands responsibility and brings plenty of headaches. Remain innovative and don't be discouraged at setbacks.

Success brings its own rewards—both monetary and personal.

PILOT BOOKS READING SHELF

PROFITABLE PART-TIME, HOME BASED BUSINESSES. Shows how to make additional money from a part-time business requiring a slight investment. All the enterprises fulfill legitimate community needs. The amount of time and commitment required is flexible and may be expanded or retracted to fit the needs and abilities of the individual. $2.50

HOW TO TURN IDEAS INTO DOLLARS. You may be sitting on top of a fortune and not realize it. This book provides you with a formula for creating profitable ideas and then shows how to market them. $2.50

SMALL BUSINESS IDEAS FOR WOMEN-AND HOW TO GET STARTED. This guide to the field of self-employment provides information on businesses which can be started with a modest investment; many that can be operated from the home on a part-time basis. You are shown how to get started, how to promote your business and given a description of small business opportunities especially suited for women. $2.00

HOW TO MAKE MONEY SELLING AT FLEA MARKETS AND ANTIQUE FAIRS. Shows you step-by-step how to get started and how to cash in. Covers what to sell, where to find merchandise, finding out about the shows, pricing, setting up your display and selling techniques. The final result, once you've learned the ropes, is a profitable small business of your own. $2.00

STARTING AND OPERATING A PLAYGROUP FOR PROFIT. A guide to a small business from your own home. If you are the sort of person who really enjoys small children, then this book will show you how to turn play into pay. A Playgroup is a business that can be started on a limited budget, either full or part-time. Learn how to turn an enjoyable pastime into a profitable business. $2.95

Pilot Books   347 fifth avenue, new york, n.y. 10016

As in all Pilot Books, this compact volume gives you quick insight into subjects of far-reaching importance. The material covered is stripped of time consuming and wasteful verbiage. You receive only the vital information you need to make important and correct decisions.

The Publishers